Mel Bay's First Lessons

Drumset

by Frank Briggs

CD CONTENTS			
1	Introduction		Metronome Tracks
2	Patterns 1-4	18	♩=60
3	Patterns 5-8	19	♩=70
4	Patterns 9-12	20	♩=75
5	Summary 1-4	21	♩=80
6	Introduction 1-4	22	♩=85
7	Proper Position 4	23	♩=90
8	Adding Rests 5-8	24	♩=100
9	Patterns 9-12	25	♩=105
10	Patterns 13-15	26	♩=110
11	Proper Position	27	♩=115
12	Patterns 2-5	28	♩=120
13	Patterns 6-9	29	♩=125
14	Patterns 10-13	30	♩=130
15	Patterns 14-17		PlayAlong Song
16	Summary 1-4	31	With Drums ♩=80
17	Summary 1-4	32	Without Drums ♩=80
		33	With Bass ♩=80

It doesn't get any easier.....

1 2 3 4 5 6 7 8 9 0

Visit us on the Web at www.melbay.com — E-mail us at email@melbay.com

Introduction

First Lesson was written with the beginning drummer in mind.

Designed to help the student develop 3 part coordination skills between the snare, hi hat and bass drum.

First Lesson will help you set up your kit, hold your sticks properly, and play a blues style song.

Playing music can enrich your life and bring countess hours of enjoyment to you and your listeners.

I hope you will find this introduction inspiring enough to continue your education in music.

About the Author

Frank Briggs is a musician, teacher and clinician in the Los Angeles area. He has currently written several drumset instructional books and DVD available from Mel Bay publications and your local music store. His credits include international and domestic touring and recording with various artists as well as commercial and corporate projects.

Practice Suggestions

Remember all tempos are valid; practice the exercises at all tempos.
Use the metronome tracks provided on the CD to help you develop good time.

Endorsements

Frank plays:
Paiste Cymbals
Attack Heads
DW Pedals & Hardware
Noble & Cooley Drums
Regal Tip Sticks
E-Pads

Acknowledgements

Special Thanks to: William Bay, Tom Shelley, Jim Bickley, Michael Hakes, Rich Mangicaro, Eric Paiste, Joe Viscardi, Jay Jones, John Good, Don Lombardi, Attack, Paiste, Noble & Cooley, DW, Mark Nelson, Guitar Center, Sam Ash, Drum Studio, Mars Music, Long Island Drum Center, Drome Sound, Tom Lee Music, Shure Bros and J.C.

Credits

Recording, lay out and design by:
712 Media, Los Angeles, CA
Recorded: November 2001

Web Resources

www.melbay.com
www.frankbriggs.com
www.iplaymusic.tv
email questions or comments to:
firstlesson@frankbriggs.com

Books by Frank Briggs

Easy Beats & Breaks (Book/CD)
Essential Reading (Book/CD)
The Complete Modern Drumset
(Book / DVD / VHS Video)
The Good Foot (Book/CD)
Drum Set Dailies (Book/CD)
Funky Beats & Breaks (Book/CD)
First Lesson (Book/CD)

First Lesson - Contents

Metronome Tracks

	Tempo	CD Track
Click Track	♩ = 60	18
Click Track	♩ = 70	19
Click Track	♩ = 75	20
Click Track	♩ = 80	21
Click Track	♩ = 85	22
Click Track	♩ = 90	23
Click Track	♩ = 100	24
Click Track	♩ = 105	25
Click Track	♩ = 110	26
Click Track	♩ = 115	27
Click Track	♩ = 120	28
Click Track	♩ = 125	29
Click Track	♩ = 130	30

Play Along Song

	Tempo	CD Track
With Drums	♩ = 80	31
Without Drums	♩ = 80	32
With Bass	♩ = 80	33

First Lesson - Key to Notation

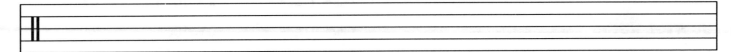

Crash Cymbal

Bass Drum

Hi Hat Cymbals

Snare Drum

Toms: Hi - Mid - Floor

This is 1 empty measure or bar of music.

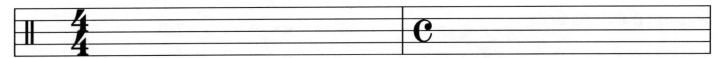

Here is the same measure with a time signature specified.

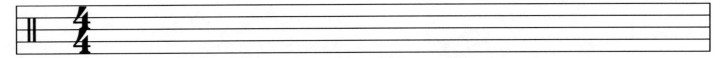

The top number stands for the number of beats in the measure and the bottom number indicates what note value is to receive the beats. In this case there are 4 beats to the bar and the quarter note (or rest) will receive one beat. 4/4 is also known as common time because it is the most common time signature and may also be represented with a C.
This is the only time signature (or meter) that we will be using in this lesson.

♩ = 60 bpm (tempo marking)

Music also has a tempo or "speed" that is indicated in BEATS PER MINUTE or bpm.
For instance 60 bpm is one beat per second and moves in the same speed as the second hand on a clock.
A note value also needs to be specified and is usually the quarter note though theoretically any note value could be used. So what is the common form of indicating the tempo of a piece of music?

♩ = 60 bpm or ♩ = 120 bpm etc. which means the quarter note moves at this tempo.

These speeds can be called up on a musician's tool called a "metronome".
An average metronome will click or beep to whatever tempo is set.
There are many different types of metronomes on the market.
I have included several different metronome tracks on the CD for you to practice with.

First Lesson - Key to Notation

♩ = 60 bpm

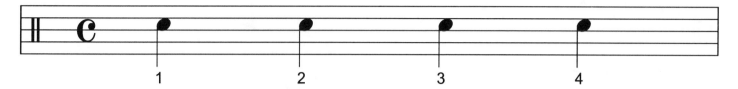

We are all pretty familiar with how a ruler works.
A measure of music works in much the same way only it has sound
The quarter notes above divide the measure of 4/4 into 4 equally spaced sounds.
In this case it is a snare drum but could also be applied to a piano or other instrument..

A NOTE is a character that represents a duration of rhythmic sound.
A REST is a character that represents a duration of silence.
Every note has an equivalent rest.

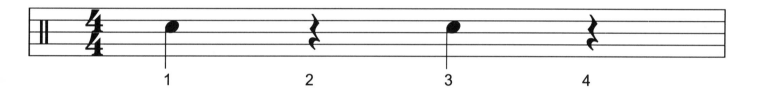

In the example above there are 2 quarter rests.
(see the glossary for a complete list of notes and rests)
The rests are counted and have the same duration as a quarter note only they are silent.

This orderly series of pulsations or combination of sound and silence is called rhythm.

Repeat Sign

A repeat sign is used when one wants to indicate that a measure is to be repeated.
In the instance of a repeat sign the student would go back to the beginning of a measure or phrase
and play it again and usually only once unless indicated otherwise.

For our purposes in this lesson you should repeat all exercises until you are comfortable with them.

First Lesson - Key to Notation

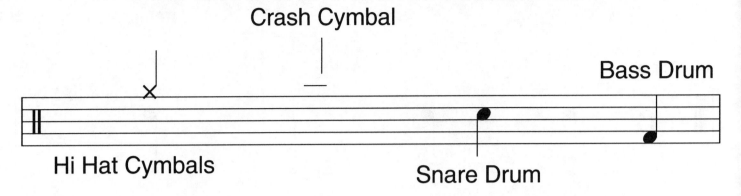

Crash Cymbal

Bass Drum

Hi Hat Cymbals

Snare Drum

Notes are set on different lines and spaces of the music staff to represent different voices of the drum set in the same way they would represent different tones on a piano.

Notes may be played in a horizontal order like the measure above or in a vertical fashion like the measure below where more than one voice on the drumset is played at a time.

This is the basis of independence on the drum set

First Lesson - The Drum Set

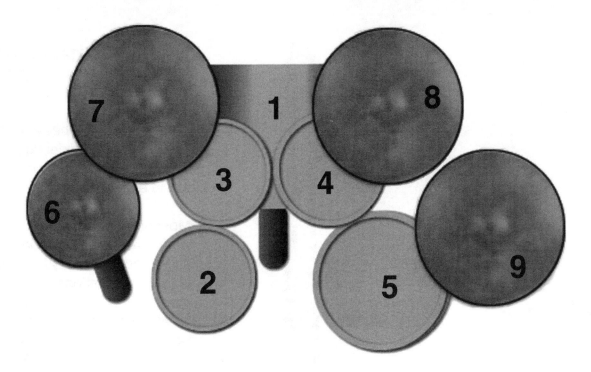

- 1. Bass Drum
- 2. Snare Drum
- 3. High Tom
- 4. Mid Tom
- 5. Floor Tom
- 6. Hi Hat Cymbals
- 7. Crash Cymbal
- 8. Ride Cymbal
- 9. Crash Cymbal

The above diagram illustrates the proper position of a standard 5 piece drum set.

In our first lesson we will focus primarily on the bass drum, snare drum and hi hat cymbals only. This is to help the student develop solid time keeping and 3 way coordination before adding other elements of the drum set.

First Lesson - The Drum Stick

Tip >

Shoulder >

Shaft >

Butt >

Starting with the proper stick is very important to the beginning drummer.

A stick that is too heavy or too long can hinder the student's progress and could cause physical discomfort in extreme cases.

Most of the drumsticks made in the world are made of wood and my suggestion to the day one student is that your first pair of sticks be made out of wood. The most popular wood sticks are made from Hickory. Other types of wood used to make sticks include Oak, Maple and Birch. I once owned a pair made from Rosewood that were intended for practice only.
My personal preference is Hickory because it seems to give a little and isn't real heavy like most oak sticks tend to be. The average drum stick is about 16" long

My suggestion for your first pair of sticks is to buy a pair of 5A or 5B. For the younger student or someone with small hands I would suggest a 5A or even 7A (which is smaller in length and diameter) to start with.
I use Regal Tip 5A and 8A sticks exclusively.

First Lesson - Grips

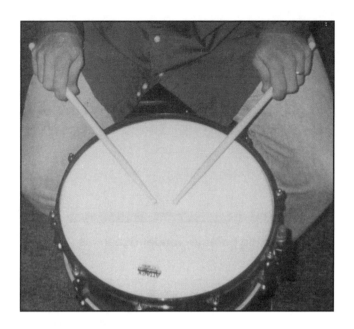

Matched Grip

Hold the stick between the thumb and first joint of the index finger about 1/3 of the way up from the butt end. Lightly wrap the remaining fingers around the stick and turn your palms toward the floor. This is my preferred grip for most drum set applications.

Traditional Grip

(left hand only): Place the stick between your thumb and index finger and between your middle and ring finger. The fulcrum or balance point (about 1/3 up from the butt end) should be between your middle and ring finger.

Matched Grip - Palms Up View

Traditional Grip - Palms Up View

First Lesson - Strokes & Dynamics

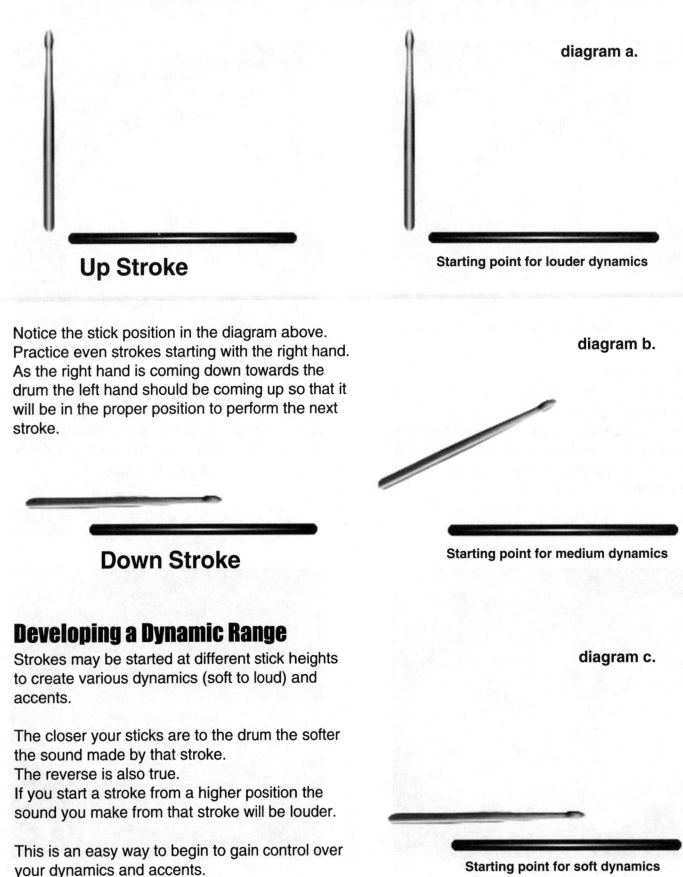

diagram a.

Up Stroke

Starting point for louder dynamics

Notice the stick position in the diagram above. Practice even strokes starting with the right hand. As the right hand is coming down towards the drum the left hand should be coming up so that it will be in the proper position to perform the next stroke.

diagram b.

Down Stroke

Starting point for medium dynamics

Developing a Dynamic Range

Strokes may be started at different stick heights to create various dynamics (soft to loud) and accents.

diagram c.

The closer your sticks are to the drum the softer the sound made by that stroke.
The reverse is also true.
If you start a stroke from a higher position the sound you make from that stroke will be louder.

This is an easy way to begin to gain control over your dynamics and accents.

Starting point for soft dynamics

First Lesson - Note Values

Whole Note

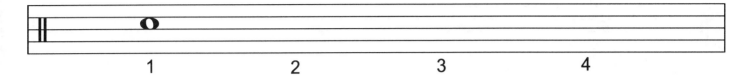

1   2   3   4

Half Notes

1   2   3   4

Quarter Notes

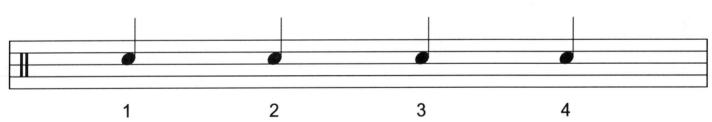

1   2   3   4

Eighth Notes

1   and   2   and   3   and   4   and

First Lesson - Snare Drum Study

Quarter Notes & Quarter Rests
On the Snare Drum

Track #2

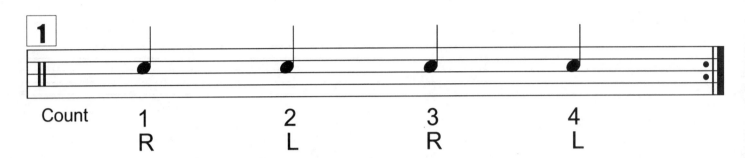

Count   1   2   3   4
         R   L   R   L

Quarter Notes and Quarter Rest Combinations

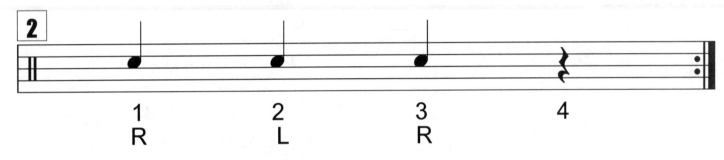

1   2   3   4
R   L   R

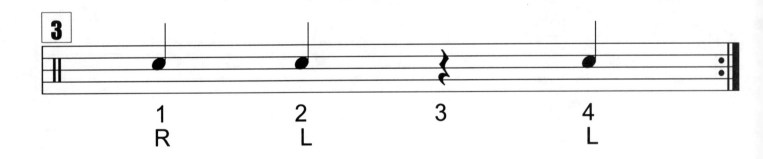

1   2   3   4
R   L   L

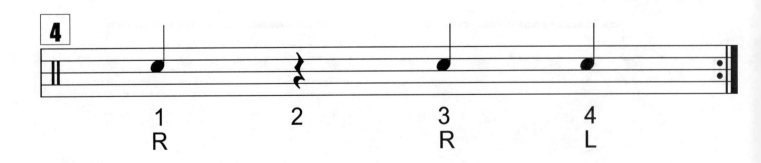

1   2   3   4
R   R   L

First Lesson - Snare Drum Study

 Track #3

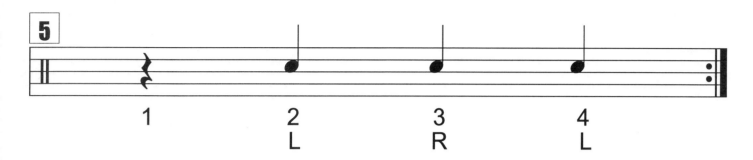

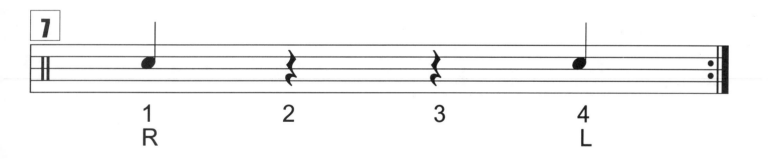

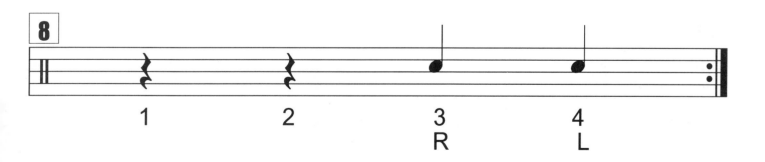

Quarter Notes

First Lesson - Snare Drum Study

 Track #4

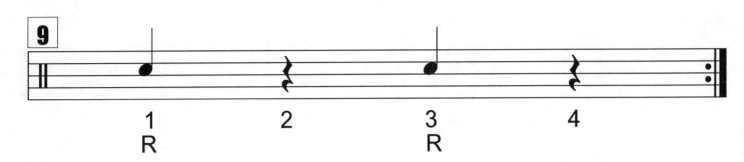

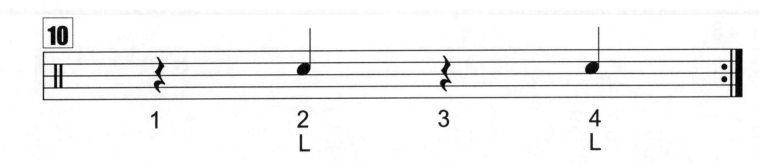

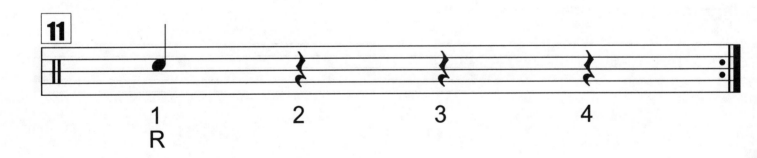

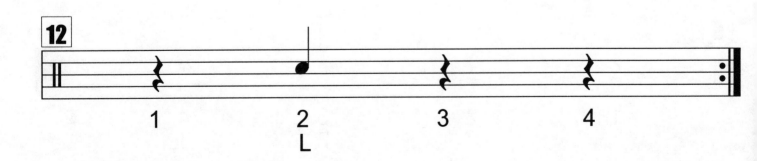

First Lesson - Drum Set

Syncopation

Here are some 4 measure quarter note and quarter rest exercises. Notice that by adding rests and longer phrases we start hearing more musical sounds in our drumming

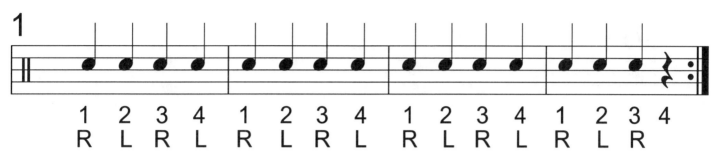

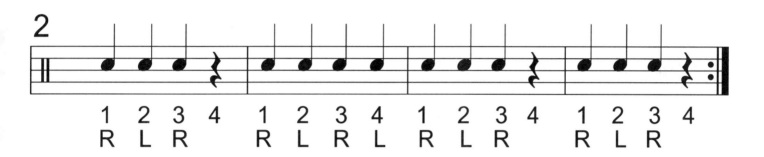

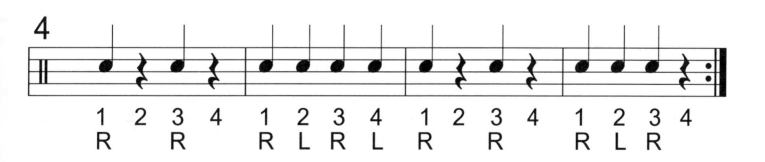

First Lesson - Drum Set

Adding the Bass Drum

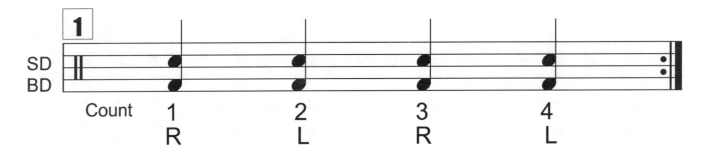

Now that you have completed playing quarter notes and quarter rests.
Let's kick it up a notch by adding the bass drum to the mix.

The above exercise may be broken up if you are having difficulty at first as it is written.

Try playing the right hand and bass drum (example 2).

Then the left hand and bass drum together (example 3)

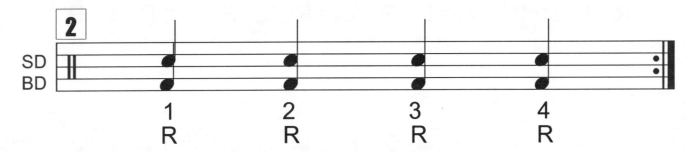

Count out loud while you are playing these exercises.

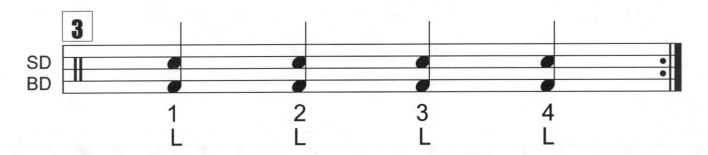

Once you have finished exercises 2 and 3 go back to exercise 1 and practice it with the metronome tracks on the CD. If you or your teacher feel you are comfortable with exercise 1 and are able to keep yourself aligned with a metronome track you may now continue through this section.

First Lesson - Drum Set

Adding the Bass Drum

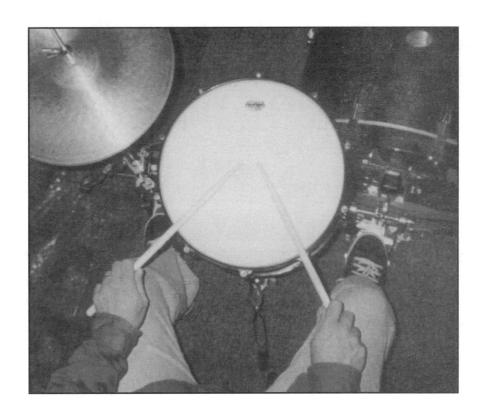

 Track #7 **Proper position of hands and feet**

Adding the Bass Drum

First Lesson - Drum Set

Adding the Bass Drum
and rests

Track #8

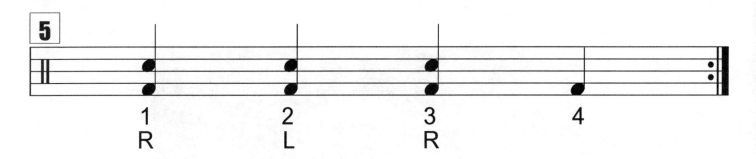

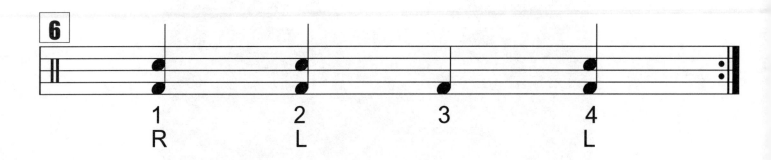

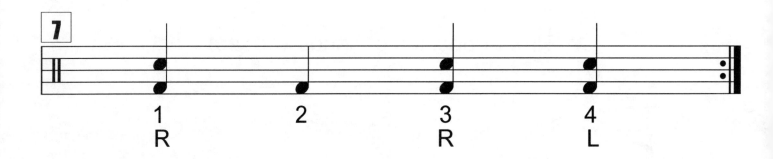

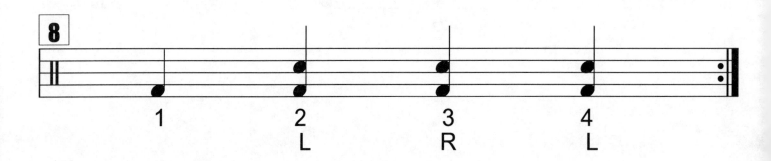

First Lesson - Drum Set

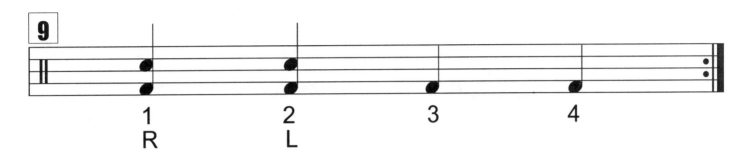

9

1   2   3   4
R   L

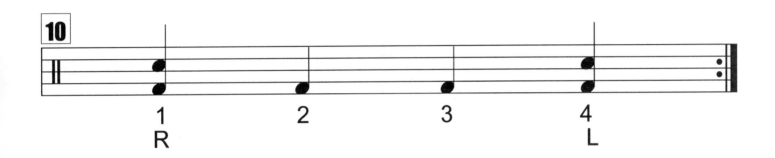

10

1   2   3   4
R   L

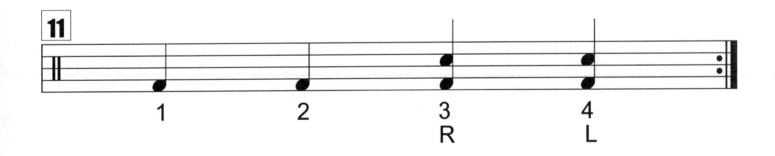

11

1   2   3   4
              R   L

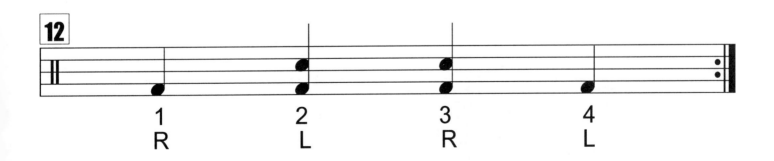

12

1   2   3   4
R   L   R   L

         Adding the Bass Drum

First Lesson - Drum Set

 Track #10

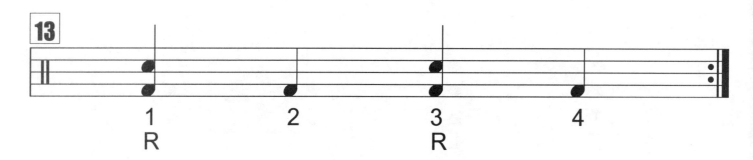

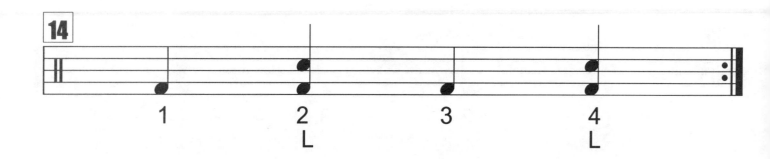

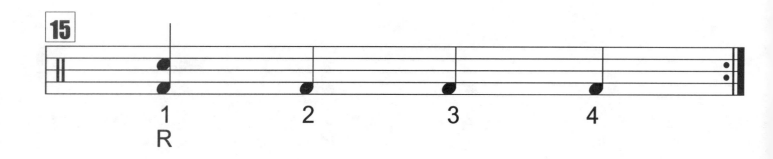

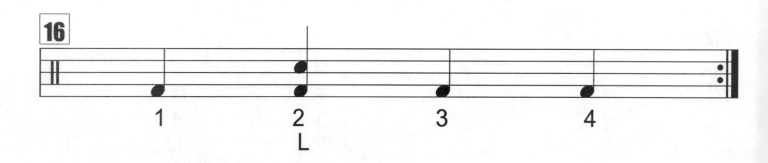

First Lesson - Drum Set

Adding the Hi Hat

 Track #11

Proper position of hands and feet

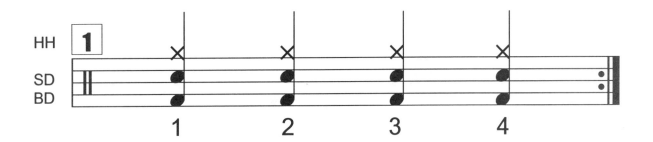

21

First Lesson - Drum Set

 Track #12

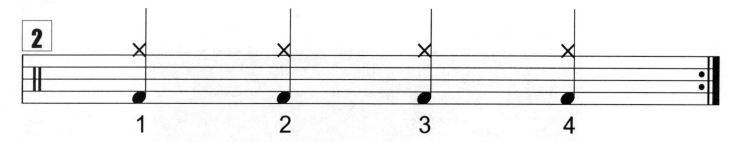

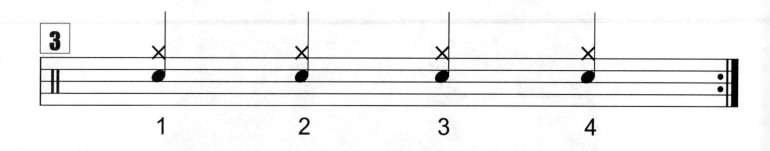

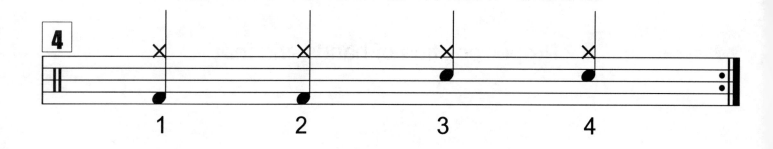

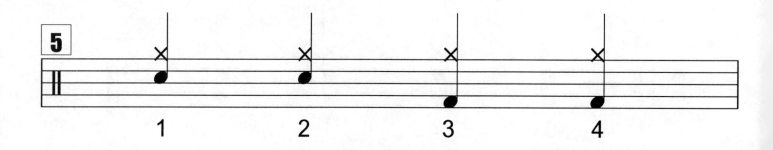

First Lesson - Drum Set

 Track #13

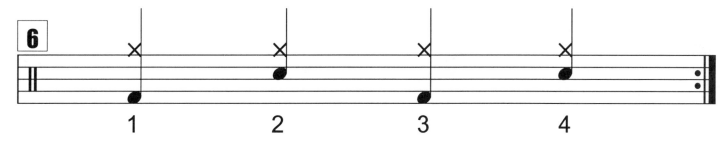

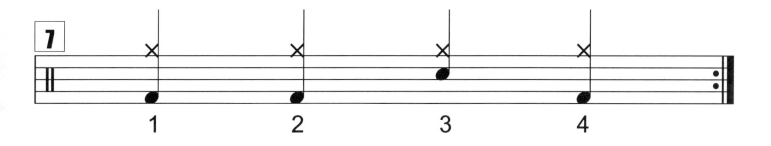

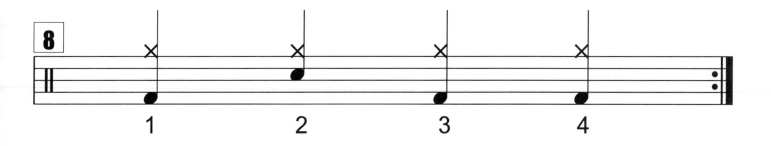

Adding the Hi Hat

First Lesson - Drum Set

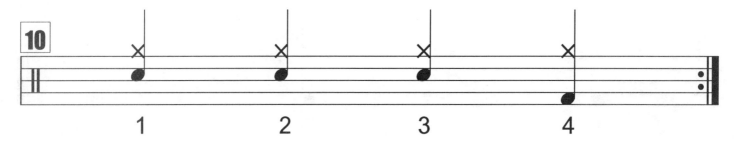

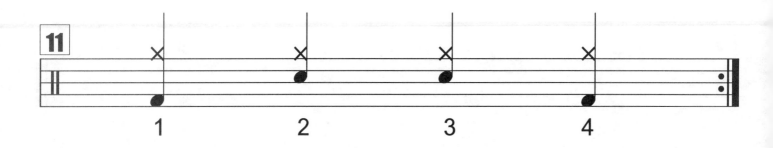

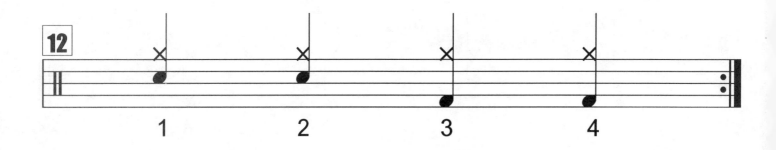

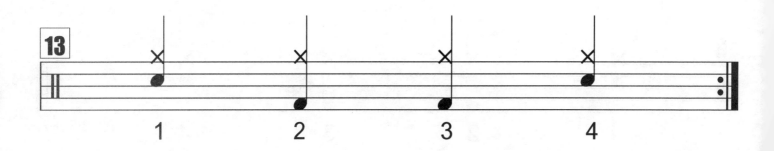

First Lesson - Drum Set

 Track #15

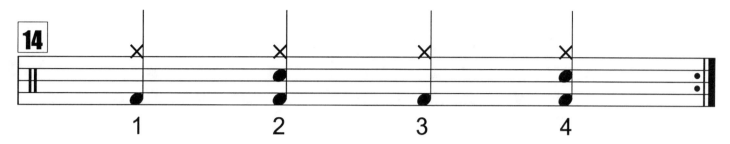

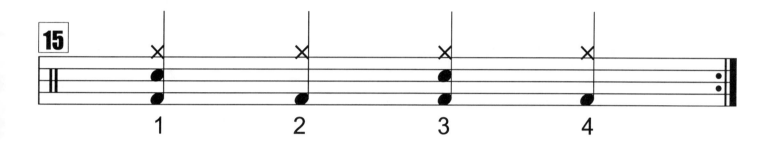

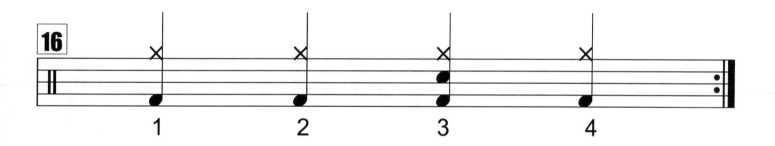

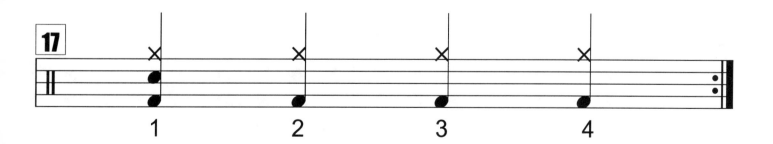

Adding the Hi Hat

First Lesson - Drum Set

4 measure beat exercises

Track #16

Play along song

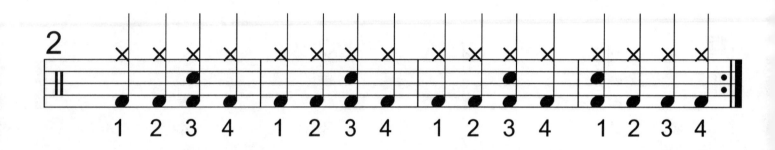

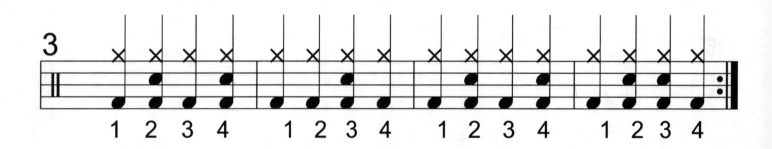

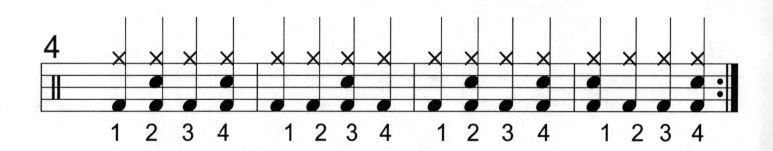

First Lesson - Drum Set

4 measure beat exercises
with crashes

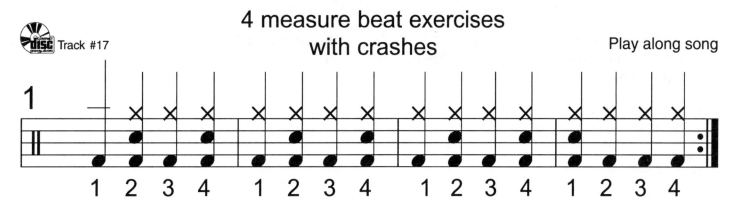

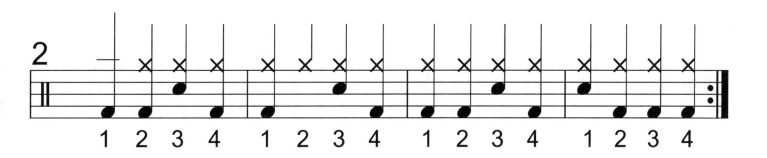

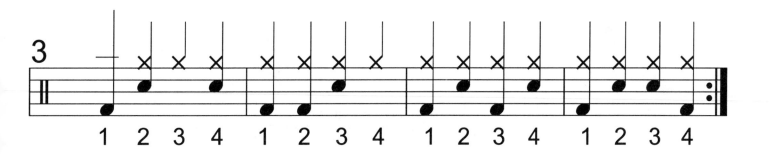

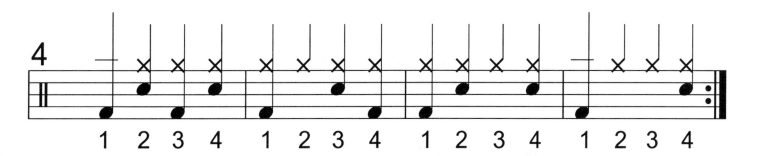

Drum Set Summary

First Lesson - Glossary

NOTE : A character that represents the duration of rhythmic sound
REST: A character that represents the duration of silence.
Every note has an equivalent rest.

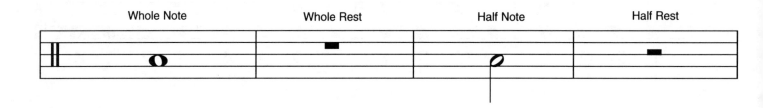

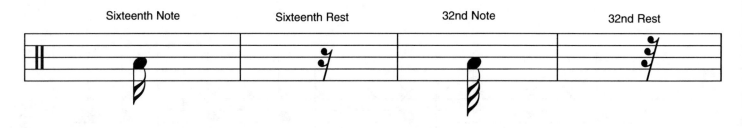

DOTTED NOTES & RESTS
A dot placed after a note or rest increases the duration of that note or rest by 1/2...
EX: a dotted 8th note is equal in space to an 8th and one 16th.

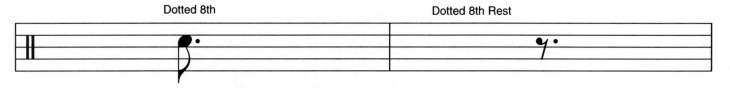

DOUBLE DOTTED NOTES & RESTS
2 dots after a note or rest increases the duration by 3/4...
EX. a double dotted quarter is equal in space to a quarter and 3 16th notes.

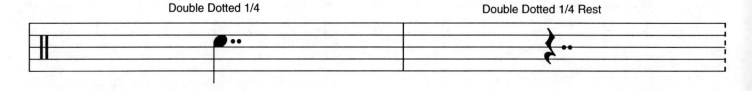

First Lesson - Glossary

FERMATA (HOLD)

This sign placed over a note or rest means that the note or rest is to be held beyond it's normal value.

ACCENT

A note with this sign over it is to be played with more emphasis or louder (accented)

TIE

A curved line connecting 2 notes of the same pitch. The second note is not played, it's duration is added to that of the first note.

TIME SIGNATURE

The top number is the number of beats in the measure. The bottom number is the note value that receives one beat.

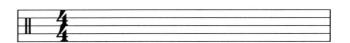

COMMON TIME

Same as 4/4 time.

CUT TIME

Also called double time. A quarter note becomes a half note.

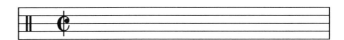

SIMILE

in the style or spirit of...

PLAY (8)

(or any number) an abbreviation for compressed rests

First Lesson - Glossary

CRESCENDO
Increasing in volume.

DECRESCENDO
Decreasing in volume

DAL SEGNO (or DS sign) 𝄋
The sign you return to in a DS.

𝄋 <<<---Return to the sign   **D.S.**

CODA
This is another sign usually used in
conjunction with a DS or DC
and a TO CODA, this allows a skipping
over of a portion of the chart
EX. DS to coda or beginning to coda.

REPEAT SIGN
This sign means
repeat the previous measure.

REPEAT SIGN
This sign means repeat the previous
2 measures.

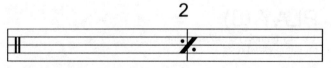

First Lesson - Glossary

REPEAT MARKS

A pair of double dotted bars means that the music between these marks is to be repeated once.

METRONOME MARKING

EX. quarter note equals 120 bpm.

♩ = 120

D.C. al Coda

From the beginning to the coda   ⊕

D.C. al Coda

D.S. al Coda

From the D.S. sign to the coda   𝄋 ⊕

D.S. al Coda

D.S. al Fine

From the D.S. sign to the end.   𝄋

D.S. al Fine

D.S.

To the Dal Segno sign   𝄋

D.S.

Fine

The End

Fine

To Coda

To the coda sign   ⊕

To Coda

First Lesson - Glossary

D.C. al Fine
From the top to fine.

D.C. al Fine

DC
To the Top

D.C.

MULTIPLE ENDINGS
At the end of a section of music there may be more than one ending, and they can contain any number of bars. After repeating the section substitute the second ending for the first the third for the second etc.

1.   2.   3.

SLASH MARKS
are used to indicate fills or time playing...

RIGHT THIN DOUBLE BAR
Indicates the end of a section.

RIGHT DOUBLE BAR
Indicates the end of the entire piece of music.

PAUSE SIGN
Indicates a short stop or pause in the music usually conducted.

DRUM ROLL

ROLL